The Yorkshire Ridings

The Yorkshire Ridings

Watercolours by John Tookey   Words by Pete Morgan

Gordon Fraser · London

First published 1987 by
Gordon Fraser Gallery Ltd, London and Bedford
Illustrations © Gordon Fraser Gallery Ltd
Text © Pete Morgan

BRITISH LIBRARY CATALOGUING IN PUBLICATION DATA
Tookey, John
    The Yorkshire Ridings.
    1. Yorkshire—Description and travel
    I. Title   II. Morgan, Pete
    914.28'104858   DA670.Y6
ISBN 0 86092 095 X

The quotation from *Letters Home* by Sylvia Plath, edited by Aurelia S. Plath,
which appears on page 42 of this book, is reprinted by kind permission of
Faber and Faber Ltd. The poem 'Between the Heather and the Sea' from
A Winter Visitor by Pete Morgan, which appears on page 8, is reprinted by
kind permission of Secker and Warburg.

Text set by August Filmsetting, Haydock, St Helens
Colour origination by Adroit Photo Litho Ltd, Birmingham
Printed by The Roundwood Press Ltd, Kineton, Warwick
Bound by Hunter and Foulis Ltd, Edinburgh
Map drawn by Hanni Bailey
Designed by Peter Guy

Contents

Tan Hill, 56

Richmond, 18

Downholme, 19

NORTH

Staithes, 22

Whitby, 23

Robin Hood's Bay, 51

Bainbridge, 34

West Witton, 36

Aysgarth Falls, 55

RIDING

Beck Hole, 57

Sutton Bank, 46

Helmsley, 52

WEST

Kettlewell, 39

Scarborough, 50

Kilburn, 14

Byland Abbey, 44

Pateley Bridge, 53

Fountains Abbey, 29

Hovingham, 45

Malham Cove, 35

Easingwold, 13

Castle Howard, 54

Appletreewick, 38

Sutton-on-the-Forest, 15

Threshfield, 2-3

The Strid, 40

Knaresborough, 21

EAST

Carleton, 31

Bolton Priory, 41

Harrogate, 20

Lothersdale, 30

Earnhill, 17

YORK, 11 & 60

RIDING

Haworth, 27 & 28

Saltaire, 25

Beverley, 26

Cullingworth, 16

RIDING

Heptonstall, 42

Bradford, 32

Howden, 48

Kingston-upon-Hull, 58

Halifax, 43

Goole, 47

Patrington, 37

Redbrook Colliery, 12

Holmfirth, 24

N

Spurn Head, 59

Rotherham, 49

Sheffield, 33

0   20 Miles

0   30 Km

Introduction

I am a 'foreigner' to Yorkshire. I was born in Leigh, in Lancashire, and
nothing is more foreign to a Yorkshireman than that.

My introduction to the neighbouring county came early. One Sunday
afternoon when I was about six my mother sat me down with my
grandfather's photograph album. I found one picture I really liked; a
sepia print of the pantile roofs of ancient cottages. Behind the roofs
there was a storm at sea and in the foreground washing billowed on the
line. But what really fascinated me was the name written in white ink—
'Robin Hood's Bay'. I already knew the legend of my hero but I had
never heard of the village. My mother was in the kitchen. 'Where's
Robin Hood's Bay?' I shouted. 'It's in Yorkshire and it's falling into the
sea,' she replied. 'It's in the North Riding.'

I didn't understand the word 'Riding' but somehow a mysterious
magic was created. Years later I visited the county and explored each of
the three Ridings—the 'thirdings' of Yorkshire—and I came to love
each one for its particular quality of life and language. I decided I
wanted to live in Yorkshire but which Riding to choose? I settled for
the independent heart of the county, York.

My home was a flat in Coffee Yard, off Stonegate, above what used to
be a public house. There was nowhere to sit outside but in summer the
sun beamed through the skylight and tempted me out. Out, onto the
motorbike—a 500 cc Norton built like a one thousand. In York it was
easy riding—North or West or East.

I visited Lancashire and there were many different routes to take.
Sometimes I roared away over the top, the A59, through Wharfedale
into Airedale, climbing back to my native county. Sometimes I stuck to
the B roads through an alphabet of villages—Airton, Bedlam, Cracoe—
and other times I chose the major roads through the industrial heart of
the West Riding. After the visit to the old abode I always felt a sense of
release when I paused at the boundary, high in the Pennines, and
looked down on my adopted home. Two wheels soon gave way to
four but I couldn't see much from behind the wheel and settled for a
convertible. The top was down in every kind of weather to intensify
the senses. Even, one day beside the River Wharfe, in the rain. It looked
good, sounded good and raised the scent of Granny Hoods and
Lilybind.

It wasn't always wheels which made the climb across the Pennine
range. I walked and clambered once. Then, one day, over twenty years
after I had moved to Yorkshire, the Regional Manager of BBC Television
North asked me to say which way I had *never* made the journey and

how I would *like* to travel? 'By water,' I told him knowing it could be done. 'Then let's go all the way from the Irish Sea to the North Sea,' he said. That journey took me on a new circuitous route, a voyage *underneath* the Pennines, through Foulridge Tunnel, past Farnhill, Kildwick and Saltaire. When we got to Leeds (surely the twentieth-century administrative capital of Yorkshire) we took the Aire & Calder Navigation to the Port of Goole. Then on to the Ouse and the River Humber until we reached what used to be called the German Ocean. On that particular exploration I was not alone. A film crew was with me and we hoped that if we did justice to the voyage, the viewers would accompany us in their millions. I couldn't be selfish. I couldn't simply look at those things which interested me—the bookshops, the pubs, the village characters. This time I included the buildings, churches and cathedrals, the changing landscape, the natural history. Even though I acted as the guide I learned a lot about Yorkshire I had never known before— geology and geography! I thoroughly enjoyed myself. Who wouldn't? To have the time to travel through the largest county in Britain by water—true luxury.

All of that happened a long time after I had become a full-time writer in 1969 when I was by no means certain that I could earn my living from my pen *and* continue to live in a county town. So I returned to my first love—Robin Hood's Bay. That three-mile stretch of shoreline is typical of Yorkshire; full of change from the sea level 'dock' in the one-time smugglers' village to the 600-foot heights of what was once a Roman signal station, (just one link in a chain of shoreline observation posts which reached from Carr Naze, near Filey, to Goldsborough, north of Whitby). I found I wrote about the place and the titles of the new poems reflected its multiformity—'Gouge', 'Hill Path', 'Oil', 'Gorse', 'A Little Hymn to Alcohol'. Sometimes they echoed the Yorkshire language—'Cheggies' (chestnuts), 'Felty' (the fieldfare, the winter thrush). But it wasn't just the landscape which provided the stimulus for new work—what I used to call inspiration! People were also there, the friendly and unfriendly:

> Between the heather and the sea
> A slipshod curve of arable and scree
> Climbs from the sea to seeping moor
> Where in between the neighbourly
> And not so neighbourly close doors
> Against the winter wind, the sleet,
> The dull necessity of speech.

I have travelled the poetry reading circuit from John o' Groats to Land's End, spending as much as a week on reading tours in different counties. Some I loved—Devonshire and Gloucestershire and Cornwall—but in each case the natural beauty of those places seemed more or less the same from end to end. I looked back on my adopted county and I looked back on variety—the windswept sweep of the North York Moors, the sheltered sublimity of the Dales, that remarkable haggard coastline which stretches, with its change on change, from the village of Staithes to the tip of Spurn Point.

After the local government reorganisation in 1974 I was no longer able to look back on the Yorkshire Ridings. The readjustment of the boundaries had given away little bits of each of the 'thirdings' to Cleveland, Durham, Humberside and Lancashire. Thankfully it failed to remove the word 'Riding' from the English language—in Yorkshire they call a spade a spade—and despite the administrative jiggery-pokery Yorkshire did remain the largest county in the British Isles.

To the Southerner, who never ventures so far north, the place frequently tends to be thought of as a music-hall joke—all mills and mines and steelworks—the land of the stand-up comic! Or as some kind of industrial mausoleum. That particular misrepresentation is partly due to the work of those Yorkshire novelists who helped create the 'Angry Young Man' of the 1950s—John Braine in 'Room at the Top', Stan Barstow in 'A Kind of Loving'. And it is probably because of the films of those novels that the picturegoer tends to remember the immediate environment of the place of work and dismiss the surrounding landscape—those moments when Joe Lampton and Vic Brown were able to escape from the humdrum workaday world to the natural beauty on the doorstep.

It is impossible to look at the Yorkshire Ridings without an element of literary pilgrimage. The traveller cannot possibly visit Haworth and be unaware of the Brontë sisters and shades of *Wuthering Heights* while in each of the three there are reminders of Winifred Holtby, the creator of the fourth—*South Riding*, published after her death in 1935 and a Yorkshire novel in a class of its own. Somehow the 'aitch' of Holtby is a pointer to the county's contribution to various arts in the twentieth century. There's Hughes, the Poet Laureate. Hockney, the painter *par excellence*, and Hutton on Yorkshire's pride of place, the pitch! Now Yorkshire no longer drops its aitches and even an adopted son takes on one in his pseudonym—James Herriot, the writer whose fame is used in the selling game, as tourists are beckoned to 'Herriot Country', the north-east corner of the Dales.

Literature is hidden. The church dominates. Throughout Yorkshire the ecclesiastical architecture pierces the skyline as a reminder of the power and the one-time wealth of the Church of England while the Non-conformist Chapel upholds a certain modesty to prove that faith is not displayed *without* but held *within*. In the old towns the chapels are not immediately obvious and need to be discovered—the Oldest Methodist Chapel in the World at Heptonstall in the West Riding and one of the most magnificent in England at Patrington in the East. Both chapels lie within the shadow of a dominant tower, a boastful spire.

The biggest county in Britain is too large to be explored in a round trip and it is geographically impossible to begin in the south, head north, and take in everything. If the traveller sets his foot in the heart of the county every place in *The Yorkshire Ridings* is a one-day journey there and back, a circuitous dog-leg of a route which takes in the change of landscape, history and trade. Not every traveller treads his path like that. Frequently a one-day trip is sufficient—to Aysgarth Falls or the City of Sheffield. That's always true of the Yorkshire coast. One sees the sea and tends to stick with it.

Over the years I have worked with many fellow poets. The field of poetry is as diverse as the landscape of the Ridings. It embraces the ancient and the modern, the free form and the strictly controlled. Each poet's eye will differ in its chosen point of view, its individual mood. It is the same with the illustrator. These days the photographer rarely takes just one picture. He clicks away and picks the best. One shot is rarely good enough! John Tookey has managed to capture the spirit of a place in one illustration. But unlike the photographer (and more like the poet) he is able to shift a doorway, a chimney pot, a tree to record the essential quality. It is left to the individual explorer to venture through the ginnels and the alleyways for the quiet surprises of the place. Looking at the Yorkshire Ridings through John Tookey's pictures I became intrigued by the towns and villages he has chosen to reflect his viewpoint—from 'Little Germany' in Bradford to 'Winter in West Witton'. I began to look with his new eye and discovered other sides to the Yorkshire Ridings. Undoubtedly that is the main fascination of my chosen home, my county. For twenty-five years I have explored Yorkshire. I do not know it all and never will. It changes character mile upon mile.

Low Petergate, York

The city which gave the county of Yorkshire its name is called 'the second city of England' and the fact that York *is* a city can never be forgotten. Each ginnel, each snicket, each alleyway, each road appears to converge on the Cathedral, the largest Gothic church in Northern Europe—the magnificent York Minster.

The place where the Minster stands has always been the site of York's most important building. The Principia, the Roman military headquarters, once stood at the end of Petergate. Those who walk the bustling street with the overhanging buildings toward the magnesium limestone of the bell-towers are pacing what was once the Via Principalis, the main cross-street of the Roman fortress of Eboracum.

Fifteen hundred years after the Roman occupation substantial fragments of Roman York remain and the impact of the Viking invasion is still reflected in the names of the streets—Fossgate, Goodramgate, Gillygate, Stonegate. The ending 'gate' is Scandinavian, the same as the Swedish 'gatan' and the Danish 'gade'—a street.

In Viking speech the name of the city was shortened from 'Eboracum' to 'Eoforic' then to 'Iorvik' and 'Jorvik' and finally to the single barking syllable of York, a name which doesn't quite reflect the elegance of the place; but a name which has travelled the Atlantic and settled in New York, New York.

Old York, Yorkshire is a revelation. There is something here for everyone, whatever the interest. From the birthplace of Guy Fawkes (in 1570) to the tomb of Dick Turpin (dated 1739). From Northern Ale in the oldest public house, the Olde Starre Inn in Stonegate (1644), to Yorkshire-grown zucchini in the traditional daily market.

In 1584 the balladeer William Elderton, 'he of the ale-crammed nose', wrote a twenty-two verse ballad with a repetitive chorus to let it be known that York was also his second city:

Yorke, Yorke, for my monie,
  Of all the citties that ever I see,
For mery pastime and companie,
  Except the cittie of London.

Redbrook Colliery, Barnsley

Ask any visitor to describe the working heritage of Yorkshire and it is a safe bet that the rural nature of the county will be forgotten. The answer will be wool, and steel, and coal. These days the Lawrentian landmark of the pit-head wheel isn't easy to find but at Redbrook the past survives, surrounded by the future. Right next door to the old is the new—a £23m redevelopment where the collier's trade is modernised but not hidden. In Barnsley they keep to tradition, take a certain pride in the past.

Originally the mining of Yorkshire coal was done by private enterprise but on January 1st 1947 a new flag was hoisted over every colliery and a notice was hammered on the coal mine gate—'This colliery is now managed by the National Coal Board on behalf of the people'. Almost forty years later the name was changed to 'British Coal' but in Barnsley they don't go along with that. They tend to stick to 'NCB'.

Those who pass by Redbrook on the surface are unlikely to suspect the twenty-foot shaft beneath, which leads to a network of subterranean flood-lit roads where the coal is conveyed a couple of miles to Woolley. The latter is well-known for its output, 619,000 tonnes a year, and a previous employee—Arthur Scargill.

A Corner of Easingwold

Stick to the A roads and some of the towns and villages in Yorkshire give the wrong impression. That's certainly true of Easingwold where the northbound A19 becomes Long Street and creates a by-pass to the real town centre.

In the coaching era Long Street was an important staging post for the Royal Mail but these days the driver has no time to note the listed buildings, the Flemish bond brickwork, the decorated chimneys.

Turn off Long Street, down Chapel Lane to the marketplace and the real Easingwold is revealed. The original shop fronts and the Westmorland slate of the rooftops are all clues to the history of the town.

In 1086 the Domesday Book recorded that there was a church in 'Eisincewalde'. Today from the churchyard below the fifteenth-century spire of St John's, one of Yorkshire's best known man-made landmarks can be seen on Roulston Scar—the White Horse of Kilburn. The Kilburn horse was originally carved into the natural limestone but Kilburn's most famous son was a carver of a different sort—Robert 'Mousey' Thompson. Inside the Easingwold church the trademark of the Thompson mouse adorns the high altar and surrounding panelling. They are difficult to find without a torch but they are there—just as they are in Westminster Abbey.

Kilburn

In summer the village of Kilburn can be as busy as a town. The horse and the mouse are the main attractions. On the most congested days it is the villagers' good fortune that houses are set back from the road. Each plot of land keeps visitors at bay! But those who live in the terraced row can't fail to understand why people come—they see it from their windows every day. They look out over the Thompson workshops—with showrooms which would grace a city—and over the stacks of weathered oak which dot the village. The central cottage describes the other point of interest. The name is 'White Horse View'.

In 1898 *Gentlemen's Magazine* described the horse on the hillside. 'The whole of the profile . . . covers three roods of ground and to fence him round would enclose two acres'. The measurements—314 feet in length, 228 feet high—were not recorded but it was stated that thirteen men could sit on the one eye. However the horse is best seen from a distance—twenty miles on a good clear day.

By contrast the Thompson mouse is tiny—inches from the tip of tail to whiskers. Robert Thompson died in 1955 but his work is carried on by one-time apprentices. Be warned! The Thompson showrooms are *not* open on a Sunday. Wise!

Sutton-on-the-Forest

Despite the occasional overhanging trees the first impression of Sutton-on-the-Forest might be that the place has lost the forest! In fact the word had a different meaning when the village got its name. At that time 'forest' was not only woodland but also an area reserved for hunting as the name of this particular forest clearly demonstrates—'Galtres' or 'Galtresse' meaning 'boar's brushwood'. Such was the power of the hunt that the wild boar is no longer with us. Now the village is surrounded by arable farmland but the hunt survives. In June the pheasant abound and the hunter no longer shows his skill with the arrow but with gunshot.

In the church of All Hallows hang the names of all the incumbent vicars from 1160. To the non-ecclesiastic the most notable name is Laurence Sterne, the author of *Tristram Shandy*, vicar until 1768. By that time he had won the fame he once said he was writing to achieve. Opposite All Hallows lies the privately owned Sutton Park with the eighteenth-century hall and high-walled gardens. To look through the iron gateway is to look on the work of another famous name— 'Capability' Brown.

Viaduct near Cullingworth

The railway mania of the 1830s and 1840s has left at least one considerable mark on Yorkshire—the criss-cross gridiron on the map where 'The Permanent Way' once ran before the nationalised conglomeration of British Rail, before the infamous Beeching Plan. At Cullingworth the stone survives. Here a viaduct which carried one of the most memorable lines in railway history dominates the valley. On a windy day the view can spur the fertile imagination. The huff of cloud above the arches brings back the memory of steam.

Steam is never so far away in Yorkshire. In the old West Riding the Worth Valley Railway, opened in 1867, runs from Keighley to Oxenhope. In the North Riding the North Yorkshire Moors Railway runs the steam to Pickering and the Middleton Railway, authorised in 1758 and said to be 'The Oldest Railway in the World', survives to run its short journey from Hunslet into Leeds.

Thanks to George Hudson, 'The Railway King', the city of York became the northern centre of the railway empire in the nineteenth century. Now, the National Railway Museum attracts a million visitors each year but the old lines in the old Ridings also attract the travellers —the Settle/Carlisle line is, in scenic terms, the Best in Britain.

But it's also good to walk, where the track returns to nature, across the valley at Cullingworth with a bird's eye view from The Queensbury Line of the old Great Northern Railway.

Farnhill

These days not everybody explores Yorkshire by road. Some prefer water. One of the best approaches to any settlement has to be to travel by boat. Somehow the view from water-level provides a new outlook on a town. But the most revealing approach of all is found on the man-made waterway. Now there is the double image; the reality of stone and mortar, and the reflection in still water.

At Farnhill in the Airedale Valley, the steep streets spill down the hillside to the banks of the Leeds & Liverpool Canal, the longest canal in Britain and one of the most significant industrial developments of the eighteenth century. Here the width of the canal provides the reflective magic for the traveller. Each house in Main Street seems to turn its back on the road and present a new façade to the waterfront.

Farnhill lies on one of the longest uninterrupted stretches of the Leeds & Liverpool—seventeen miles from lock to lock—and here the water goes *over* the road, across the single-span Kilburn aqueduct. Thanks to the lack of any interference by man a 200 year-old monument to Yorkshire's industry has now become a linear corridor carrying wildlife and plant life almost to the heart of Leeds. Thanks to the constant water-level in a waterway cut by man the Leeds & Liverpool has become far more protective toward flora and fauna than the rise and fall of the River Aire, the river which gave the valley its name.

[17]

Richmond

The city of York takes a modest pride in shipping the placename across the Atlantic. Richmond holds the record. The name has travelled to over fifty places throughout the world—to America, Australia, New Zealand.

In 1071 Count Alan Rufus built himself a castle on the crag overlooking the River Swale. He took the name from the Old French 'riche mont' ('rich' or 'royal hill'). Rufus became Earl of Richmond and 400 years later another Earl of Richmond came to the throne as King Henry VII. He built himself a palace near London and the travels of the name began—from Richmond, Yorkshire, to Richmond-on-Thames.

The Norman castle still dominates the cobbled marketplace which was once the outer defensive bailey. But the castle never experienced attack and the township gathered around the wooden palisades. Now the perimeter of the bailey is marked by the circle of shops and houses which skirt the market square.

In the middle ages Richmond ranked as one of the chief market towns in northern England. It is still a working place, with its busy market on Saturdays, but the town holds on to its history through the castle, the market cross, the Georgian Theatre in Friar's Wynd and 'Hill House' once the home of Frances I'anson, the 'Lass of Richmond Hill'.

A different kind of history is never far away. At Downholme the official tourist map provides a curt description of the surrounding moorland—'Military Training Area'.

Downholme

Royal Pump House, Harrogate

In Victorian England the spa town of Harrogate had no equal with over eighty mineral springs full of health-giving properties. The Royal Pump House, built in 1842, epitomises the elegance of the time but the style persists throughout the town—in the Royal Hall and the Royal Baths Assembly Rooms, boasting the Turkish Bath.

The Harrogate spa water came in four different varieties and from the Royal Pump gushed the most potent of the lot—'strong sulphur'. It certainly is 'strong', not too strong to taste but strong enough to flavour the air out on the greensward of the Stray—the 200 acres of well-cropped grass which encircle the town in horseshoe shape.

Thanks to the restriction on new building even the modern reflects the Victorian in the mirrored walls of the 2,000 seat Harrogate Conference Centre and the fourteen-storey International Hotel. 'Once inside,' says the blurb, 'you'll quickly discover that sumptuous living has reached new heights in the twentieth century.'

Back outside the history of the town remains intact—preserved in the shops and offices, the hotels with their wrought-iron canopies, and in the Royal Pump House now the Museum of Local Antiquities. Although it is no longer a spa Harrogate is a museum in itself. It is firmly lodged halfway between the ancient and the modern, halfway between elegance and efficiency, halfway between the capital cities of England and Scotland—a sort of dead centre—but very much alive and twitching. Lodged in the middle of everything and still it has no equal; it is not like anywhere else in Yorkshire.

Misty morning, Knaresborough

Four miles from the stolid Victoriana of Harrogate the ancient town of Knaresborough straddles the morning mists of the River Nidd. Apart from the castellated viaduct there is no similarity between the two places. It could have taken a hundred miles to get away from that to this! Here the early morning mood is somewhat Elizabethan with the ruin of Knaresborough Castle dominating the gorge. By lunchtime, on a summer's day, the mood has changed from Elizabeth the First to Second— or at least to the people of her realm. There is ice-cream, candy-floss and booze!

It is surprising that a town with a population of under 10,000—one sixth that of Harrogate —can boast six times the history: in the medieval cobbled square; the Norman church of St John the Baptist; the four-poster bed used by Cromwell; the 'Oldest Chemyste Shoppe' in England, and Mother Shipton's cave. Born Ursula Sonthiel in 1448, Mother Shipton was a phenomenal soothsayer. In the Knaresborough dialect she foresaw the Victorian gentry sipping their sulphur-laden water, the erection of the viaduct across the Nidd and the day when the peat-moss of Harrogate was transformed into a town:

When lords and ladies stinking water soss,
High brigs o'stean the Nidd sal cross,
An' a toon be built on Harrogate moss.

Staithes

The best view of Staithes is from the sea. To watch the fishing village's huddle of cottages from the rise and fall of the prow of a coble provides an exhilarating impression of pantile roofs clustered round the gully of Staithes Beck. Care is necessary despite the break-waters protecting the dock. The tide's reach can be treacherous and three times in history a wild sea has ripped away the Cod & Lobster Inn.

To look at the staggered undulation of the cliffs and crags is to witness the variety of the Yorkshire coastline—a shaft, a wyke, a nab, a knock; all aptly named on the 1:25,000 map. The only thing they don't have here is sand, no golden reaches of the stuff like Scarborough and Bridlington. But Staithes was never a holiday resort. It has always been a working village.

Whitby

In the village of Staithes a plaque on a cottage wall commemorates the lodging house of a thirteen-year old boy. In Whitby, ten miles along the coastal road, the same boy is commemorated in manhood with a life-size statue on the West Cliff overlooking the harbour—'Captain James Cook, 1728–1779'. In Whitby Cook learned the craft of navigation which made him one of the world's most celebrated explorers and one of Whitby's most famous adopted sons. Other sons are fact, some fiction.

Fact? Caedmon, the cowherd-poet whose life is commemorated in the memorial cross close to the top of the 199 steps leading to Whitby Abbey—'The Father of English Sacred Song. Fell asleep hard by, 680'.

Fiction? Count Dracula! In Dracula's case the original story has become somewhat denigrated by the visual media's search for loud red blood but Bram Stoker's novel is decidedly underrated. It contained some vivid description of Whitby: 'The houses of the old town... are all red-roofed, and seem piled up one over the other anyhow... The harbour lies below... one long granite wall stretching out into the sea... an elbow crooked inversely...'

Stoker's novel was first published in 1897 at a time when another celebrated son (by adoption) practised the craft which had already won him fame—the photographer, Frank Meadow Sutcliffe, who captured turn-of-the-century reality with his remarkable photographs of goat-bearded men and bonneted women. When *Dracula* first came out the book sold over a million copies and it still sells quite steadily. So do Sutcliffe's photographs, kept on view in the Sutcliffe Gallery in Flowergate.

Holmfirth

After the three Ridings of Yorkshire (the 'thirdings') were rearranged, Holmfirth found that it belonged to a new Metropolitan Borough Council. An English Tourist Board mini-guide proclaims the area's identity—'Kirklees: The Real Yorkshire!'. It's not wrong (as Yorkshiremen frequently say when something is right), after all, the area does cover 160 square miles and among the towns of Kirklees are well-known Yorkshire placenames typified by brass bands, Rugby League and beer—Huddersfield and Dewsbury and Batley.

If this part of 'Real Yorkshire' has a capital which (as they say) Yorkshiremen 'favour' it must be Holmfirth where the old town nestles in the Holme Valley flanked by hills and moorland. The change in the name of the area has failed to change a town with a distinct appeal recognised by the visual arts. The town guide makes a claim: 'This small area of the Pennines probably has more successful working artists ... than any other comparable part of Britain'. Most of the artists are 'foreigners' but Holmfirth has always been the home of Bamforths, the printers famed for their saucy comic cards of bathing belles and breeze and knickers—'Come on in, the water's lovely!'. Recently the visual appeal of the valley has reached an even wider audience thanks to the power of television—and Nora Batty!

Saltaire

The canal age brought the first 'new town' in Europe to the Aire Valley. Saltaire—the dream-town of Sir Titus Salt, one-time Liberal MP and Mayor of Bradford.

By 1850 Sir Titus had made his fortune from his mills. Instead of retirement he bought land conveniently situated on the banks of the Leeds & Liverpool Canal and commissioned architects to build a mill and a new town to his specification. Sir Titus' aesthetics resulted in a model community in sandstone—850 houses, a public baths, an infirmary and the fourteen-acre Saltaire Park complete with statue of the benefactor.

The mill itself was grandiose—at the time the largest in the world and designed to all the highest contemporary standards, with internal air-conditioning and external mock Italian Renaissance (the result of a rare concern for the visitor's point of view). Thankfully the eye does not immediately take in the ageing of Sir Titus' factory and only after some scrutiny does the verse by Vachel Lindsay come to mind:

Factory windows are always broken.
Other windows are let alone.
No one throws through the chapel window
The bitter, snarling derisive stone.

North Bar Gate, Beverley

Five hundred years ago Beverley was deemed to be the 'second' city of Yorkshire. Today the link with York is unofficially maintained by 'The Minster Way'—a 51-mile walk between the two great Minsters. The walk might take a couple of days, at least! Drive it, along the more direct route—twenty-nine miles along the mundanely named A1079 and A1035—and it takes just forty minutes, at the most!

Beverley (once 'Beferlic', 'beaver brook') is a remarkable town and the Minster rivals that of York with a West front reputed to be one of the finest examples of Gothic architecture in Europe. Outside, fourteen ornamental pinnacles pierce the skyline. Inside, a 1,000 year-old fridstool, a chair of peace, once afforded sanctuary to fugitives.

The interior of the nearby church of St Mary rivals the Minster. Founded in the twelfth century St Mary's contains an example of startling modernisation. The chancel ceiling is adorned with portraits of the Kings of England, first painted in 1445, but in 1939 the legendary Lucrine was obliterated and replaced by a smiling portrait of King George VI. St Mary's has a literary connection—Charles Lutwidge Dodgson visited while staying with friends. The sight of the sacristy guarded by a carved hare with a satchel on the shoulder inspired him to invent the Mad March Hare when he wrote under the pseudonym Lewis Carroll.

Head north, toward the A164, and the 'old town' ends where the North Bar Gate stands between classic Georgian houses. The shape of the 10' 9" arch (restored in 1409 at a cost of £96 9s 11½d) has made its mark on twentieth-century transport—the local double-decker buses were once designed with arch-shape roofs so they might safely pass beneath it. Today the same necessity for safety makes passage through the gate a one-way traffic. When the red lights change to green the traveller finds that present-day Beverley doesn't stop! Beyond the gate is the racecourse, said to be the 'prettiest' in England. But the North Bar *is* a gateway. Keep to the A164 for a while, turn left, stick to the B roads, and the surrounding sweep of sweet chalk pasture provides one of the county's least explored but most rewarding regions—the Yorkshire Wolds.

Haworth

Those who catch the steam train of the Worth Valley Railway at Keighley can leave the train at Haworth and climb the steep uneven street where the Brontë family haunt the village.

Today a colony of artists produce a seemingly limitless output of Brontë scenes but these have changed considerably since Charlotte described the place as 'the little, wild moorland village'. Many of the houses the family knew are still there but many have become shops and cafés marketing their Brontëana—Brontë biscuits, Brontë Liqueur and, of course, Brontë books.

Thankfully the original Brontë landscape is never very far away and the distant moorland can provide a feeling of profound release. In her poem, 'Amid the Barren Hills', Emily Brontë described 'A little and a lone green lane/That opened on a common wide ...'. Climb the cobbled hill to find that lane—no longer quite so green or little. It runs from the church alongside the Parsonage to the lonely moorland, the 'Wuthering Heights'. Here are the miles of heather, bilberry and bracken which inspired the sisters to exaggeration.

Haworth Parsonage

Members of the local civic society in Haworth have kept their eye on new developments to ensure that those intrusions which cater for thousands of visitors don't affect the character of the place. They've done quite well. The more commercial temptations remain discreetly hidden behind the windows and the walls of houses.

The devout literary pilgrim to Haworth climbs the cobbles to the building overlooking the graveyard and the church of St Michael and All Angels. Here the blackish millstone grit gives way to the Yorkshire sandstone of the Parsonage—a museum administered by the Brontë Society for over fifty years.

Inside, many of the rooms are kept as the Brontës must have known them, displaying the family relics—the children's toys, their clothing,

the father's spectacles and pipe, the pistols kept for self-defence but never used apart from practice shots across the moors. A new wing houses the Bonnell collection of manuscripts bequeathed from Philadelphia. To the visiting writer the collection is a revelation. It seems they got it right first time! Almost!

Despite the rebuilding of the church in 1881, twenty years after the father, Patrick Brontë, died, St Michael's preserves the Brontë connection with the collection of ecclesiastic furniture used in the family's lifetime. Even the Black Bull Hotel, where Branwell did his apprentice drinking, is proud to boast of the lad's temptation which contributed to his eventual failure in the arts. Small wonder, with such remarkably talented sisters as Charlotte, Emily, and Anne.

Fountains Abbey

Thanks to the size of the county there are more monastic ruins in Yorkshire than anywhere else in Britain. Not only are they 'most' in quantity but also the most magnificent. At one time Fountains Abbey was the richest and most powerful Cistercian monastery in England. Now it is the finest floodlit ruin.

These days the setting is tranquil but the monks who selected the site in the twelfth century found it 'a better lair for wild beasts than for human beings'. In winter, when the snow has fallen, the place is a hark back to the past through isolation, stillness and muffled peace. In spring it comes alive again through greenery and then the eighteenth-century preservation becomes more obvious in the surrounding grounds of

Studley Royal Park—the 650 acres of woodland, deer park and ornamental garden created as some form of classical compensation for the Abbot, hanged after the Dissolution, and the ruin that Henry VIII created.

After the Dissolution the stone, the glass and the lead were taken. There is less than a quarter of it left but it doesn't take much effort to visualise what must have been a glorious interior—the immense vaulted cellarium still stands, as do the stone coffin in the Presbytery, the inscribed bands on Archbishop Huby's tower and the lofty elegance of the Chapel of the Nine Altars.

Lothersdale

Carleton

Carleton and Lothersdale are a couple of miles apart as the high-flying crow flies, double that if you go by road—as different as cod and carp! Those who would prefer to look at a less commercialised region of Brontë country should visit Lothersdale, and go in winter, in the snow. It was here, in the house called Stone Gappe, that Charlotte Brontë took on the role of governess. In *Jane Eyre* she changed the name to Gateshead Hall:

I leaned against a gate, and looked into an empty field where no sheep were feeding, where the short grass was nipped and blanched. It was a very grey day; a most opaque sky, 'onding on snaw', canopied all ...

Carleton inspired a somewhat different kind of writing. Toward the end of the sixteenth century a petition was sent to the landowner:

Carltoun is verray barrayne grownde for gresse and pasturadgre, by reason of the hyllie ground and hie lyinge of the same, yet frewtful for corne.

Lothersdale and Carleton are not major tourist centres and it seems they have no desire in that direction. They keep their secrets under lock and key. Down in the mill at Lothersdale, founded in 1792, is the largest waterwheel in England. To stand beside it is to learn what Tom Thumb must have felt when he clambered into the woodman's cart and rode away in the horse's ear.

Little Germany, Bradford

Thanks to the avaricious demands of the motor car the Victorian image of most of England's city centres has been destroyed by streamlining and modernisation. Today the parked cars in the sidestreets of 'Little Germany' might provide something of an interruption to the Victorian air but owing to the comparative remoteness of the area, and the Civic Amenities Act, that heritage survives in Bradford, once the wool capital of the world.

The City of Bradford became what it was because of where it stood—in a natural basin surrounded by rising ground and sheep! When the industrial revolution covered the hills with mills and robbed the sheep of grazing ground the city began to import its raw material from anywhere and sell the finished cloth to everywhere—the glory of Queen Victoria's England!

In layman's ears the term 'Victorian' might possess a somewhat patronising tone suggesting an element of artistic debasement, but forget the sidestreets and 'To Let' notices and take a closer look at the quality of the masonry, the evidence of the stonecarver's art, and the warehouses which provide one of the most impressive examples of Victorian Britain.

There is no absolute evidence to indicate when the placename of 'Little Germany' was first used but it is known that German names once appeared on almost every building. One of the names passed into English musical history—Frederick Delius, a son of Yorkshire.

Paradise Square, Sheffield

Stainless steel has made Sheffield one of the best-known placenames in Britain. The trademark on the knife blade simply gave the maker's name, the place, the nation. The name of the county was rarely recorded but visit the city, look at the tumble of hills which provided the grindstone and the rivers which provided the power, and there is no doubt it's Yorkshire.

The first impression of the city centre is predominantly twentieth century because of contemporary architecture. But in Chaucer's *Canterbury Tales*, written in the fourteenth century, the Reeve describes the Miller:

He had a Sheffield dagger in his hose.
Round was his face and puggish was his nose...

New buildings in Sheffield frequently fake such antiquity but in Paradise Square the truly ancient is preserved. Thanks to the slope of land on which the city stands Paradise Square became a somewhat theatrical meeting place. The best-known visitor—John Wesley.

Bainbridge

Malham Cove

As far as the number of visitors is concerned Malham is the most popular village in the Dales. There is Malham Tarn, the highest lake in the Pennine range, 1,000 feet above sea level; and Malham Cove, the sheer-faced semi-circle of overhanging rock, 300 feet from the lowest point to highest.

Leave the village of Malham and the first view of the Cove is impressive—the vertical white cliff of limestone dwarfs the dark greenery of the trees. The direct route to the top makes demands on the climber. For the walker the path leads up the Western side where a flight of steps prevents erosion by trampling feet. The steps still call for a degree of huff and puff but the most spectacular view is from the top—the aerial view of the tiny stream, the beginning of the River Aire, burbling at the limestone base.

Malham Cove is well-visited by geographers, geologists—and writers! In 1858 Charles Kingsley looked down from the top of the Cove to the infant river and noted the black marks made on the cliff by lichen. The black marks made him think of soot and inspired the fantasy of the chimney-sweep boy who clambers down the face of the rock and joins the source of the river—the beginning of 'The Water Babies'.

Winter, West Witton

Dales winters can be hard and they always seem long—from the back-end of autumn through to spring when the visitors return to let the Dalesman know the hard part of the season's over.

The ardent detective can always spot the village where winter is not forgotten. The clue is in the curl of smoke unlicking from the chimney pots. But one of the smokiest days in Wensleydale happens late in August, on the Saturday after St Bartholomew's Day—the West Witton Feast and the Burning of Bartle.

The effigy paraded and burned is thought to represent a local outlaw who once haunted the forest above the village while its name is probably a corruption of the name of the Patron Saint of the church. The ancient chant is shouted through the village:

In Pen Hill crags
He tore his rags:
At Hunters Thorn
He blew his horn:
At Capplebank Stee
He brake his knee:
At Briskillbeck
He brake his neck . . .
Shout, lads, shout!

Laurence Sterne recorded the feast in his *Sentimental Journey* (1769).
'He had been flea'd alive, and bedevil'd and used worse than St Bartholomew, at every stage he had come at . . .'

Cricket at Patrington

In summer one thing is the same in every part of old Yorkshire. Venturing down the dog-leg of Holderness in what was once the East Riding the explorer might think the journey almost over. All that is left is the flat, gaunt landscape stretching miles to the mouth of the Humber. Suddenly it isn't over—there is the soaring spire of the cruciform church of St Patrick, and beneath the spire it's 'over' of a different kind. It's cricket!

Now, in the officialese language of local government, Patrington is 'Humberside'. But Yorkshire County Cricket Club stick to the ancient boundaries in their selection of the county side—the only team in England with the self-imposed rule that all who play must be born within the county boundaries.

Those who play cricket in any part of old Yorkshire remain eligible for the 'Champion County'—a term coined by Sir William Worsley in 1958 at the annual meeting of the club when Yorkshire finished up eleventh. 'We in Yorkshire know which is the Champion County, irrespective of what side happens to be at the top of the table at any one time.' The following year they got the title back.

After the match it's 'champion', as they say in Yorkshire, to visit the fourteenth-century church or to visit the nearby village of Winestead where the poet Andrew Marvell was born in 1621. Certain lines to his Coy Mistress echo the sound of Holderness:

> Thou by the Indian Ganges' side
> Shouldst rubies find: I by the tide
> Of Humber would complain. I would
> Love you ten years before the flood...

Appletreewick

Appletreewick looks wrong on the page—the placename is pronounced as 'Aptrick', just two syllables. It is, without question, one of the most delightful of the Wharfedale villages and all the better for being slightly off the beaten track.

Take the major road heading south from Kettlewell, through Threshfield into Burnsall where a minor road turns off to the left—over the bridge, two miles to Appletreewick on the quiet side of the valley.

In the green hills above the village the earliest Wharfedale lead-mining scars the landscape. A hundred years ago half the men from the village were employed in lead but the most famous son was a farmer's lad—William Craven. At the age of thirteen, in 1561, he was sent by carrier to London where, years later, he became 'Dick Whittington of the Dales', Sir William Craven, Lord Mayor of London.

Sir William did not forget his native village and came back home a wealthy man. The Craven riches were well spent. He was the man who built the road, the 'causeway' and they called it then, from Burnsall into 'Aptrick' and it was Craven cash which was used to restore High Hall at the top end of the village. The magnificent example of seventeenth-century restoration still retains the ancient staircase of polished oak and the banqueting hall with the minstrels' gallery.

Kettlewell

Those who like to look back on village life as it used to be will some-times find it necessary not to notice certain things. Kettlewell is typical. Forget the telegraph poles and the public telephone box, and the view of Gate Cote Scar above The Racehorses Hotel is much the same as it was in the past.

The various trademarks of the different breweries on the Hotel sign might have changed a few times—it is, after all, a free house—but apart from the colour of the rendering the exterior of the building has changed little since the late seventeenth-century when it housed the village smithy.

Kettlewell is one of the larger villages in Upper Wharfedale and thank-fully almost everything, apart from the church, has avoided major archi-tectural modernisation. Modest interior redecoration however does have certain advantages, particularly in accommodation, and this village, with its three public houses-cum-hotels, and various b and b, has become one of the best-equipped centres from which to explore the wilder reaches of the Dales on foot. As far as the necessary equipment is concerned there's an excellent shop, 'The Under & Over', discreetly hidden in the cellar beneath the Post Office.

After a hard day on the slopes of Great Whernside, above the village, returning to the sign of the placename, Kettlewell, brings us to the past, at least to the Anglo-Saxon version—'cetel wella', a bubbling spring or stream. And that is there as it always has been, tumbling down to join the Wharfe.

The Strid

By the time the River Wharfe reaches Barden Wood it suddenly narrows to thunder through a chasm in the rock. Ten feet deep, at the best of floodless times.

The name of William Wordsworth conjures up an image of Lakeland but Wordsworth was a universal writer. He wrote *upon* Westminster Bridge and he wrote *about* the Strid:

> The striding place is called the Strid
> A name which it took of yore:
> A thousand years hath it borne
>   that name,
> And shall a thousand more.

In his poem, 'The Force of Prayer', Wordsworth recounts the legend of the boy Romilly who attempted to stride across the Strid but was held back, in mid-leap, by a greyhound on the leash. Romilly's mother went into mourning for her drowned son:

> Long, long in darkness did she sit
> And her first words were 'Let there be
> In Bolton, on the field of Wharf,
> A stately Priory!

The legend of poor Romilly hasn't stopped the maniacal practice of leaping across the Strid. It is still impossible to look down on the surge of water at the bottom of the gorge without a sense of challenge.

Bolton Priory

When the Wharfe reaches Bolton Priory the river broadens. The stepping stones across the shallows and through the reflection of the ruin are the safest crossing point bar bridges.

The building of the Priory on land donated by the mother of the drowned boy, Romilly, began in 1150. By the time of the Dissolution the Prior could call on over 4,000 men to cut the corn at harvest time. Now the population of the area has dwindled but its numbers do increase in summer and the annual income must have risen since the Prior's time—then £400.

After Wordsworth's visit he wrote 2,000 lines about the place! The first six set the scene:

From Bolton's old monastic tower
The bells ring loud with gladsome power.
The sun shines bright; the fields are gay
With people in their best array
Of stole and doublet, hood and scarf,
Along the banks of crystal Wharf ...

He recounts the legend of the Norton family. Few of them escaped death or ruin but one boy gave his sister, Emily, a tame white doe which she took with her at night when she prayed in the aisles of Bolton Priory.

Visitors have been known to report that by the light of the moon they have seen a small, white, high-stepping animal lost among the tombstones.

Heptonstall

Below Stoodley Pike lies the village of Heptonstall. From certain vantage points the contrast between the Napoleonic monolith and the squat tower of Heptonstall church tends to make the village look low. It's not! Six hundred feet below its encroaching woods lies the Calder Valley, once the centre of the industrial revolution in textiles. When the valley began to develop—with the road, the railway and the river—Heptonstall did not. It remained a village where the main employment was home-weaving.

On one of her early visits, in 1957, the American poet Sylvia Plath recorded her impression in a letter to her mother back home in Wellesley, Massachusetts:

It is the one place in the world where I don't miss the sea. The air is like clear sea-water, thirst-quenching and cool, and the view of the spaces, unlike anything I've seen in my life ...

Sylvia Plath married the poet Ted Hughes, a native of the Calder Valley, who became our Poet Laureate. When she died, 'by her own hand', she was buried in the Heptonstall graveyard.

The Piece Hall, Halifax

When the industrial revolution developed the Calder Valley it brought red brick to Halifax. A Heptonstall wit recorded a sniping couplet but a Halifax rhymester revenged the quip by adding two more lines:

Halifax is built of wax,
Heptonstall of stone.
In Halifax there's bonny lasses,
In Heptonstall there's none.

The rhyme was right. In Heptonstall the lasses were rarely seen. They were weaving in the home. In Halifax they were out on the street—on their way to or from the mills where the weaving was done. Many were seen around the Piece Hall where the finished cloth was bought and sold, piece by piece.

The Piece Hall was opened in 1779—a rectangular building with an open courtyard and small rooms off the galleries. Today it houses an industrial museum, an art gallery, restaurants, antique shops. The original commercial purpose is kept alive with the market in the courtyard and the bonny lasses remain in evidence.

Byland Abbey

York Minster takes pride in the sixteenth-century glass of the rose window—originally unveiled to commemorate the end of the War of the Roses and the marriage of the Lancastrian King Henry VII to Elizabeth of York. Its red and white roses remain intact (despite the fire of 1984) but at Byland Abbey the glass has gone leaving one crag of masonry and a yawning gap high on the western wall. The diameter of the York window is twenty-two feet and four inches. Byland beats it!—twenty-six feet across, one of the largest circular windows known.

Sadly the grace of the past is left to the imagination but the size of the window provides a clue to the magnificence of what was once the largest Cistercian church in Britain—328 feet long, 135 feet wide across the transepts. Some other hints of the past survive—the medieval green and yellow tiles arranged in geometric patterns, the superb examples of carving.

Byland Abbey was founded in 1177 on the second choice of site. Earlier the monks had settled on the further side of the Hambleton Hills but found it too close to Rievaulx Abbey. Each was confused by the other's bells . . . 'which was not fitting and could not be endured'. They upped and left! Forty years later Byland stood to its own uninterrupted music.

Hovingham

The wooden footbridge across the gurgle of the beck is one of the distinctive features of villages close to the Howardian Hills. Beneath the black and white woodwork the brook looks natural enough. In fact they are frequently man-made—artificial conduits cut from the nearest natural flow of water.

The village of Hovingham lies on the route of the Hambleton Road, the ancient drove road which saw the passage of thousands of cattle to the markets in East Anglia. In the village church the Norman arches and a Saxon tower reveal something of the antiquity of the place.

In the eighteenth century the Worsley family chose the village as the site for the home which became better known than the village itself. Hovingham Hall is not divided from the cottages by the class barrier of acres of lawn and ornamental woodland but is entered from the village green.

The 'Worsley Arms' is one of the two local inns and the name of Worsley is much revered. In the 'Champion County' the reason is obvious—the late Sir William Worsley was the cricketing captain of Yorkshire in the 1920s and when his daughter, Katherine, married the Duke of Kent in 1961 they gave the county the first Royal wedding in York Minster for over 600 years.

Sutton Bank

The view from Sutton Bank has been described as 'one of the finest landscape views in England'—an opinion shared by Dorothy Wordsworth. In 1802 she recorded a visit in her Journal and described her view of the Vale of York, the flat sweep of rich farmland which divides the county. Dorothy had good eyesight:

Far far off us in the Western sky we saw the shapes of Castles, Ruins among groves, a great, spreading wood, rocks and single trees, a minster with its tower unusually distinct...

When Dorothy and her party descended the bank they took the steepest side on the right, leading down Whitestone Cliff to Gormire, one of the county's natural lakes.

There was no distinct view, but of a great space, only near us, we saw the wild and (as people say) bottomless Tarn in the hollow at the side of the hill. It seemed to be made visible only by its own light...

The belief that Gormire is bottomless is one of the local legends. Another claims that the Devil, riding a white horse, leapt from the top of the bank. The hole he created filled with water. The wonder is that the lake exists at all. No stream runs in. No stream runs out.

Late Afternoon, Goole Docks

At one time the Port of Goole was dubbed 'Bartholomew's Vineyard'. On a good day it is busy enough to earn the latter part of the nickname though the man himself might be forgotten. W. H. Bartholomew was proprietor of one of the leading companies of the canal age. Prior to his intervention in the 1820s Goole was a hamlet of some 400 farmers and fishermen. The town he built at the end of his canal became the most inland port in England, almost sixty miles from the sea and in its heyday one of the 'top twenty' trading ports in Britain.

Today some hint of former glory survives in the three miles of quays and nine wet docks. The cranes might not be as busy as they used to

be—what they will hold in the future cannot be guessed—but the continental atmosphere of the 'Vineyard' is preserved by the weekly sailings to France and Spain and the incoming traffic of Renault cars, going from port to parking place—some of them pushed!

The name of the man who created the port might not mean much now but one son of the port is well-remembered, better known than in his lifetime—Rcuben Chappell, the marine artist who left behind an unparalleled record of over 12,000 ships of Goole; sloops and billy-boys, keels and schooners. Twenty-seven of Chappell's marvellous naïve paintings survive in the local library. They evoke a past that won't return.

Howden Minster

The lantern tower of Howden Minster dominates the flatland at the confluence of two rivers. Head north, from the Port of Goole, take the minor road, missing the motorway. Take Boothferry Bridge across the Ouse, avoiding the M62 crossing point, and the Minster rises above the trees on the northern bank. Apart from the two bridges the view has been the same for centuries. For almost 500 years man has been able to stand on the deck of his barge or his sloop and watch the tower in the distance.

The sight of a single dominant architectural feature in a relatively sparsely populated area raises questions. Why so large a place of worship in so small a market town? Why the stark but welcoming ruin of the Chapter House, roofless for 300 years? The answer is that Howden was once the capital of Howdenshire, a vast administrative province governed by the Prince Bishops of Durham and it goes back still further. The first documentary evidence of 'Heaufuddene' occurs in the charter of 959 and an early history even suggests that the church is built on the site of a heathen temple.

When the Boothferry Bridge was opened it connected the West and East Riding and it cut the journey from the south bank of the Ouse to Howden from twenty miles to three and a half. However it proved to be of little commercial value to the town. Howden lost its through-traffic and also lost its local trade. But the bridge did bring one blessing—it saved the place from the ravages of later redevelopment and now the centre of the town consists almost entirely of eighteenth- and nineteenth-century building.

Today the majority of drivers rush past on the M62 with barely a fleeting glimpse of the lantern tower. When John Leland paused on his journey in 1540 he wrote, 'The town of Howden, the only market town of Howdenshire, is of no great reputation'. The same is true today but the town *is* worthy of more than that. It *is* ancient and it *has* survived.

Rotherham

Somehow it seems that Rotherham is one of Yorkshire's less revered settlements. Perhaps it is the name. If it was Rother*hithe* it might be more acceptable, romantic. But Rother*ham*? The name tends to conjure up the wrong impression. Unlike the Thames-side placename, 'a landing place for cattle', the Yorkshire name has nothing to do with meat. It is simply the 'ham' (the home, the farmstead) which stood on the banks of the 'Roder' a name of Celtic origin which has now become the 'Rother'.

Many towns and villages in the old West Riding suffer from the indignity of unromantic names—Cudworth, Grimethorpe, Kexborough—but visit the place and the first impression conveyed by the misnoma on the map is frequently removed.

In Rotherham the sight of the dignified parish church is enough to change the mind, the heart. Here the fifteenth-century central spire is 180 feet in height, completely re-built in the Perpendicular style on the foundations of a Norman building. Inside the church the medieval wood-work ranges from the fanciful carving of the misericord to the elegant figures on the bench-ends of the pews. The South chancel chapel was completed in 1480 by one of the town's most famous ecclesiastic sons, Thomas Rotherham, then Bishop of Lincoln, later Archbishop of York.

Perhaps the town's most exclusive boast is the bridge which used to cross the Don. Though the course of the river changed in the eighteenth century the bridge remains intact, just as it was when John Leland described it in his *Itinerary of England*—'A fair stone bridge of iiii [four] arches', and what he called 'a Chapel of stone wel wrought.' Leland's visit came just half a century after John Bokying, a local grammar school master, left 3s 4d in his will 'to the fabric of the Chapel to be built . . .'. At one time a chapel on a bridge was commonplace but the Rotherham bridge is one of only five remaining examples in the whole of England.

The abolition of the Ridings made an attempt at creativity—it made 'South Yorkshire'. Not for the first time! For centuries the inhabitants had used the name to distinguish themselves from other natural geographical areas in the county—the Dales, the Wolds, the North York Moors. In the south there was a widespread feeling, and a pride, that this part of Yorkshire was different—different in its landscape, its work, its sport, its speech. But industrial development in the West Riding partly obscured that difference. The factory and the housing estate, the spoil heap and the pithead wheel helped to hide the diversity of nature and history. Today the settlement which was once the farmstead on the banks of the River Roder is typical of South Yorkshire.

The first impression is often wrong. Look, and the spirit of the place is found.

Scarborough

The wide reach of sand can make the first-time visitor view Scarborough as a 'Wish you were here' kind of place. Either as that or as a medieval monument with the ruin of the castle high on the headland. Either as that or as a 'Kiss me quick' promenade of amusement arcades and fish and chip shops. Either as that or as a Victorian emporium with the seven-storey Grand Hotel—a room for every day of the year. Either as that or as a working fishing town with the harbour, the lighthouse, the fish market pier. Either as that or as a literary shrine—the final resting place of Anne Brontë, the birthplace of Dame Edith and Sacheverell Sitwell. And so it goes on·...

The list *is* endless but there must be something for everyone—in the bays, on the streets, in the harbour. If it's not there it could be in one of the town's three museums or in the Crescent Art Gallery housing the collection of one of the town's most celebrated sons, Tom Laughton, brother of Charles. Perhaps in one of the town's seven theatres—in the Theatre-in-the-Round where Alan Ayckbourn premieres are played to the world *before* they are played to the West End of London. If none of that's wanted, and the weather's fine, it's back to the sand to build a castle like the one on the hill and wait till the tide comes in ...

Robin Hood's Bay

An early sepia photograph, taken by Frank Meadow Sutcliffe, epitomises the visitors' first impression of the best-known village on the Yorkshire coast—the headland of Ravenscar in the distance, the huddle of cottages clustered at the bank top, the washing billowing on the 'drying ground'. (Rent, 1/- a year).

Today the view is much the same. Not quite! Now the washing hangs in colour beside 'Windyridge'. In Sutcliffe's time that cottage was set well back from the sea with a scrummage of houses protecting it from wind, and ridge! But 'Bay, as the locals call it, has lost 100 cottages in the last 200 years. Now a sea wall hems it in. It's safe! Safe from further land-slip and safe from intrusion by way of redevelopment. Now the only intrusion is tourism. Hundreds of visitors a day follow King's Beck down the Bank (1 in 3) to explore the snickets and ginnels leading to the shore at Wayfoot where once, it is said, the smugglers landed booty. What is more certain is the fishing—in 1845 forty-five boats and 130 fishermen were recorded. Today the numbers are greatly reduced but still some survive to carry on the old craft.

The placename is open to debate—all of it folklore rather than fact. Was it the last resort of the legendary hero? Was it named after the ancient forest elf, a spirit creature said to haunt graves? Nothing is proven by the romantic placename but the past is definitely proven by the place.

Helmsley

On a Sunday afternoon in autumn the market-place with the ancient market cross becomes the focal point of Helmsley. The surrounding hostelries tend to boast their names by visual motif, rather than by words—The Crown, The Feathers, The Black Swan. They certainly boast their custom and the parked cars are crammed into the square.

Venture into the sidestreets and the place is comparatively quiet. Opposite the Feversham Arms Hotel the babble of the Borobeck goes underground and appears to tumble a good hundred yards beneath the graveyard of the parish church to reappear in Castlegate, cutting the castle from the market square.

The Feversham Arms was rebuilt in 1855 by William Duncombe, Earl of Feversham, and the man is celebrated in the marketplace by the monument described in the Parish Guide as 'a splendid high Victorian Gothic monstrosity'. In the graveyard of the church the name Feversham reappears on the war memorial but the most appreciated reminder of the family lies in the grounds of Duncombe Park—'one of the most beautiful spots in Yorkshire'. A pass permitting access to the grounds is obtainable from the Tourist Information Centre or from the Feversham Estate Office. The splendid hall, built in 1713, is under restoration.

Pateley Bridge

Over 50,000 people visit the Yorkshire Dales on a typical summer Sunday—three times the number who live in the Dales National Park. On a Sunday in winter the locals have the place to themselves —almost. The more adventurous explorer might abandon his day of rest and the risk-taking back-packer might still pace out the heights of hills, sometimes more impressive in winter when the hills are muffled with snow.

Winter tourism is nothing new to Pateley Bridge. The long steep road out of the depths of the Nidderdale Valley climbs to one of the highest villages in England, Greenhow. When a branch line of the North Eastern Railway opened at Pateley in 1862 the visitor was greeted by posters proclaiming—'Little Switzerland'.

Tourist traffic helped the development from market village to market town but in Victorian England industry proved equally beneficial. The railway brought the visitors and took the quarried stone away. Not all of it left however, some was used in local building providing Pateley with a certain air of dignity and authority. In fact the architectural design and the building materials used would hardly be out of place at the other end of the now-defunct line, in Harrogate.

Castle Howard

Sometimes, when exploring Yorkshire, the driver has a sense of *déjà vu* by moonlight, a feeling he has been this way before. The truth is quickly realised—the lasting power of film and television! *All Creatures Great and Small* in the Dales, *The Railway Children* in the Worth Valley, *Last of the Summer Wine* in Holmfirth, and so on almost *ad infinitum*.

Those who drive through the Howardian Hills and catch sight of the domed silhouette of a Palladian mansion can instantly forgive themselves the feeling. Here was *Brideshead Revisited*.

The majority of Yorkshire castles were built as military strongholds. They follow the dictionary definition, 'a large fortified building'.

Castle Howard does not. This one, built at a time of peace, is large enough but in no way defended—the first architectural adventure of Sir John Vanbrugh. The place lives up to the television title. Now it is visited again and again.

Aysgarth Falls

Thanks to their geological structure the Dales boast innumerable waterfalls—Gill Force (sixty feet), Whitfield Force (eighty feet) and Hardraw Force, reputed to be the highest unbroken waterfall in England. 'Force' is the Northern word for a fall of water but in places the plural, 'falls', is needed.

At Aysgarth the tumbling thunder of the Ure descends a half mile of the river flanked by overhanging trees. In spate the falls are brackenish, and loud where water rushes the jagged steps of rock named by the geologists after the ancient name of Wensleydale, Yoredale. Yoredale Rock. After rain the falls are at their best.

Tan Hill Inn

The largest county in England brags its English record-breaking figures—the highest unbroken waterfall at Hardraw, the largest water-wheel at Lothersdale, the shortest river at Bainbridge. Not everything is proven. Sometimes, when the story is passed on, it is necessary to add 'it is reputed that so-and-so,' or 'they say that such-and-such'.

Visit the Tan Hill Inn on Bowes Moor and the truth is verified—the noticeboard at the entrance boasts the fact, '1,732 feet. The highest Inn in England'. In this case Yorkshire held the record—once! But the inn was a bite of the cherry when the county was robbed of the Ridings. Now it belongs to Durham.

Up here the sky predominates. Looking at the flat sweep of rock and heather it is difficult to imagine that this was once the home of coal—a shaft sunk in 1296, mined for 600 years. Today the sheep which dot the moorland grass are the living clue to Tan Hill's last remaining industry, agriculture. As home-base for the annual show of the Swaledale Sheep Breeders' Association, the inn maintains the Yorkshire connection. On the last Thursday in May the visitors proliferate—not only sheep but the breeders of sheep and Middlesmoor and Lofthouse Band, drowning out the bleating.

Beck Hole

The variety evident in the Yorkshire landscape is also found in the county's public houses— and in the beer they serve, CAMRA or not. Some of the pubs are worthy of a visit, whatever the Riding brew.

At Beck Hole, a comparatively tiny village high on the North York Moors, there were once two houses—the Lord Nelson and the Birch Hall Inn, on the right. Today only the Birch Hall maintains the licence, granted in full in the 1960s. Prior to that it was 'ale, porter, perry'. The Birch Hall is a typical example of the early development of the English pub when the tenant of a private house decided to become 'public'. Here the visitor sits in one room of the small hostelry and orders refreshment through the hatch from the shop next door. The village is worthy of a visit, even if the house is not entered, for the other remarkable feature of Birch Hall is a painting by Sir Algernon Newton hanging *outside*.

The Fish-docks, Hull

Hull is a city which tends to keep its talents hidden. There was a time when the maritime trade came right to the heart of the place in Queen's Dock. But in the 1920s that was dried out, filled in, and transformed into Queen's Gardens. Now Hull's traditional trade is stretched along the seven miles of waterfront and ten miles of quays, which busy the banks of the River Humber.

The luxury of city centre water is preserved in Hull Marina where the visitor can moor his craft just yards from the Ferens Gallery with the Canaletto, Hals and Hockney; and yards from the Docks Museum with the fine collection of scrimshaw—the art of carving on whalebone.

Whaling was once the principal trade, dating from the 1500s, but now Hull lays claim to the most modern fish-docks in Britain. It can also claim the most up-to-the-minute theatre. The Hull Truck Spring Street Theatre has become one of the many famed back-street attractions that need to be searched out.

There's no need to search for the longest single span suspension bridge in the world. But as with all bridges the best view is from underneath. For this, take the inland train, toward Leeds, and the view is the same as it would be from the water.

Spurn Head

Before the local government reorganisation of 1974 Spurn Head was the Land's End of Yorkshire—the last slip of land in the East Riding.

It seems somewhat portentous that the new boundaries should come into force on All Fools' Day but this strange geographical feature can hardly complain at administrative change. It is the most changeable place in England—the latest in a succession of narrow spits which have been thrown up by the waves, have lasted for about 250 years, and then been destroyed by the same power which created them.

Spurn Head has always been a menace to shipping—the first lighthouse was built as long ago as 1427—but now the cultivation of buckthorn and marram grass has stabilised the sand and shingle into dunes and the narrow peninsula which lengthens each year has become a nature reserve. It doesn't just play host to wildlife. It's host to the coastguard, host to the Spurn Head pilots and host to the only lifeboat in the British Isles that is permanently moored at sea, the busiest lifeboat on the English coast.

York Minster

The City of York never belonged to a Riding. It was always an 'island' city, an independent Diocese which provided a safe passage. Here Yorkshiremen from East and West and North could meet without inter-Riding rivalry, to appreciate their county town and praise the Minster—always there, inescapable in architectural dominance.

Today visitors come from every country in the world but still it's Yorkshire rules the roost! All of Yorkshire seems to come to York. In sun the visitors might stay outside the Minster but in the rain they tend to flock inside to admire the light of the hundred stained glass windows and aid the Restoration Fund.

Restoration has been necessary for over 150 years. The first fire in 1829, the second in 1840, the third in 1984 when the night sky was lit ten miles away and the whole world seemed to mourn. Now thanks to the generosity of many nations the South transept with the great rose window will be restored—one day.